MW01382900

The Perfect Picnic: The Top 25 Recipes for a Fantastic Spring Picnic

All rights Reserved. No part of this publication or the information in it may be quoted from or reproduced in any form by means such as printing, scanning, photocopying or otherwise without prior written permission of the copyright holder.

Disclaimer and Terms of Use: Effort has been made to ensure that the information in this book is accurate and complete, however, the author and the publisher do not warrant the accuracy of the information, text and graphics contained within the book due to the rapidly changing nature of science, research, known and unknown facts and Internet. The Author and the publisher do not hold any responsibility for errors, omissions or contrary interpretation of the subject matter herein. This book is presented solely for motivational and informational purposes only.

Table of Contents

Coleslaw 4

BLT Spread 5

Black Bean Salsa 6

Asian Deviled Eggs 7

Crab Dip 8

Picnic Salads 9

Italian Fruit Salad 10

Picnic Ready Potato Salad 11

Cowboy Macaroni Salad 12

Cucumber Salad 13

Greek Salad 14

Picnic Dishes 15

Jambalaya Kabobs 16

Seven Layer Jarred Salad 17

Ham & Cheese Melts 18

Fruit Kabobs 19

Smokey BLT 20

Hot Chicken Peppered Sandwiches 21

Tropical Rice with Fruit Salad 22

Celery and Apple Slaw 23

Sweet and Tangy Melon Salad 24

Picnic Pineapple Drink 25

Macaroni Salad 26

Strawberry Lemonade 27

Lemon Sweet Tea 28

Pink Palmer Jars 29

Picnic Mango Tea 30

Coleslaw

Ingredients

1/2 cup mayo
1/3 cup milk
1 tsp vinegar
1/4 cup sugar
1/4 tsp salt and pepper
1 package cabbage
cole slaw mix

Directions

I.   In a large bowl, whisk everything but the coleslaw mix.
II.   Add in the slaw mix once everything else is blended and coat well.
III.   Cover slaw and chill in fridge for 1 to 2 hours before packing for a picnic.

BLT Spread

Ingredients

1 package cream cheese
½ cup mayo
¼ tsp salt and pepper to taste
2 cup lettuce, iceberg
1 package bacon, bits
4 tomatoes, plum
2 scallions, chopped
1 cup cheese, shredded

Directions

I.   In a bowl, blend the first three ingredients and mix well.
II.   Add this to a serving plate and add remaining ingredients on top, serve with BLT.

Black Bean Salsa

Ingredients

1 can beans, black
1 can corn, whole kernel with peppers, drained
1 mango, peeled and seeded, chopped
¼ cup onion, chopped
¼ cup cilantro, chopped
2 tbsp lime, juice
1 tsp garlic, powder
½ tsp salt and pepper to taste
¼ tsp cumin

Directions

I.   Add everything to a bowl and blend well.
II.   Add to a Tupperware container with a lid and add to a picnic bag.

Asian Deviled Eggs

Ingredients

1 dz eggs, boiled, peeled, halved
1/3 cup mayo
1 tsp oil, sesame
2 tbsp sesame seeds, toasted
1 tsp wasabi, powder
1/8 tsp salt and pepper to taste
2 scallions, sliced

Directions

I.   In a bowl, blend the egg yolks, mayo, sesame oil and seeds (be sure to reserve 2 tsp of sesame seeds), wasabi powder and salt and pepper, blend well.

II. Spoon a little bit of the mixture into each of the egg whites and garnish with scallions and reserved sesame seeds.

III. Cover and refrigerate for at least 2 hours before packing for a picnic.

Crab Dip

Ingredients

1 12 oz cream cheese
1 cup sour cream
1 ¼ cup cheese, shredded
2 tbsp mayo
1 tbsp seafood seasoning
1 tbsp lemon, juice
1 tsp mustard
1 tsp worcestershire sauce
1 tbsp garlic, minced
1 can crab meat, drained

Directions

I. Preheat the oven to 375 °F.
II. In a large bowl, mix everything but the crabmeat and ¼ cup shredded cheese.
III. Once everything is well combined, stir in the crabmeat.
IV. Pour everything into a casserole dish and bake for about 15 to 20 minutes.
V. Remove from the oven and garnish with ¼ cup leftover cheese and bake for 3 to 5 minutes to let the cheese melt.
VI. Let it cool before adding the crab dip, put in an airtight container for a picnic.

Picnic Salads

Italian Fruit Salad

Ingredients

½ lb pasta, rotini
1 can pineapple, chunks with 2 tbsp juice
1 cup cantaloupe, cubes
1 cup grapes, seedless
1 container yogurt, peach
¼ cup sour cream
1 cup strawberries, fresh, stemmed and halved

Directions

I.   Start by cooking the pasta per the package instructions, strain.
II.   Add in the fruits (except the strawberries) and toss.
III. Pour fruit juices, yogurt and remaining ingredients over the fruit and pasta, stir to combine well.
IV.   Garnish with strawberries and pack for a picnic.

Picnic Ready Potato Salad

Ingredients

1 cup mayo
2 tbsp mustard, Dijon
¼ cup vinegar, white wine
¼ cup oil, vegetable
½ tsp salt and pepper to taste
3 lbs potatoes, boiled and cubed
½ cup parsley, chopped
½ cup onion, red, chopped
½ cup celery, chopped or sliced
1 cucumber, peeled and chopped
2 to 3 eggs, hard-boiled, peeled, and chopped

Directions

I.   In a small bowl, make the dressing by stirring the first 5 ingredients (salt and pepper) and set aside.
II. In a large bowl, add ½ cup parsley with the potatoes and gently toss.
III. Add in the rest of the ingredients, tossing to cover.
IV. Add to fridge overnight and the next morning, pack for a picnic.

Cowboy Macaroni Salad

Ingredients

1 lb pasta, ziti
1 can beans, black
1 package corn, frozen (thawed)
2 cups tomatoes, cherry, halved
½ cup onions, red, diced
3 tbsp garlic, minced
2 tbsp oil
½ cup mayo
¼ cup vinegar, red wine
1 tbsp parsley, chopped
salt and pepper to taste

Directions

I.   Prepare pasta according to package directions, strain and run under cold water. Strain one last time to rid the pasta of any extra starch.
II.   In a large bowl, add the rest of the ingredients and stir to combine.
III.   Add pasta to the bowl and combine sauce with the pasta, stirring well.
IV.   Cover and add to fridge for 1 to 2 hours before taking it on a picnic.

Cucumber Salad

Ingredients

2 cucumbers, peeled and sliced
4 scallions, sliced
½ pepper, red, chopped
¼ cup sour cream
2 tbsp vinegar, white
2 tbsp sugar
1 ¼ tsp salt and pepper to taste

Directions

I.   Add the cucumbers, scallions and chopped red pepper, toss everything together in a large bowl.

II.   In a separate bowl, add in the remaining ingredients and pour the blend over the cucumber mix.

III.   Set the salad in the fridge for at least 2 to 3 hours before adding to a picnic basket or serving.

Greek Salad

Ingredients

¾ cup oil, olive
4 tbsp lemon, juice, freshly squeezed
1 tbsp oregano, dried
½ tsp garlic, powder
½ tsp salt and pepper
1 head lettuce, iceberg, chunked
1 cucumber, peeled and diced
1 package cheese, feta, crumbled
2 tomatoes, wedged
1 can Greek olives, drained

Directions

I.   In a small mixing bowl, blend well the wet ingredients and season with salt and pepper.
II.   Add chopped iceberg lettuce to a serving plate and top with the cucumber and crumbled feta cheese.
III.   Add the tomatoes over the cheese, then drizzle vinaigrette over the salad.
IV.   Store in an airtight container in refrigerator until ready for a picnic.

Picnic Dishes

Jambalaya Kabobs

Ingredients

2 ½ tsp seasoning, creole
1 lb chicken breasts, boneless, skinless, cubed
½ onion, red, chopped
1 pepper, green, chopped
2 stalks celery, chopped
1 pint tomatoes, cherry
3 lemons, wedged or halved
1 package brats or sausages, chopped

Directions

I.   Preheat the grill and seasoning the chicken and vegetables.
II.   Skewer the vegetables and chicken, drizzle oil over kabobs.
III. Season one more time to taste.
IV.   Grill kabobs for 12 to 15 minutes, turning often.
V.   Serve with lemon wedges.

Seven Layer Jarred Salad

Ingredients

1 package bacon
1 head lettuce, chopped
1 onion, red, chopped
1 package peas, green, frozen (thawed)
10 oz cheese, shredded
1 cup broccoli, chopped
1 1/4 cup mayo
2 tbsp sugar
2/3 cup cheese, parmesan

Directions

I. Prepare the dressing first by whisking the mayo, sugar and parmesan, set in fridge until ready to serve.
II. Take the remaining ingredients and add them one at a time to a mason jar, leaving about 1/4 space at the top for dressing.
III. Add in the dressing, tighten lid and toss.
IV. Set in fridge until picnic time.

Ham & Cheese Melts

Ingredients

2 dz Kaiser buns
1 to 2 lbs ham, honey
1 lb cheese, provolone, sliced

Sauce

1 ½ tsp mustard
8 tbsp butter, melted
1 tbsp onion, minced
½ tsp worcestershire sauce

Directions

I. Preheat oven to 350 °F.
II. Slice rolls in half and add mayo to one side, then add ham and cheese.
III. Add assembled sandwiches to a baking sheet.
IV. Fir the sauce, mix everything together and whisk well.
V. Drizzle the well-blended sauce over the tops of the sandwiches (sliders).
VI. Cover baking sheet with aluminum foil and bake for 8 to 10 minutes.
VII. Remove foil and cook for 1 to 2 more minutes.
VIII. Serve warm or pack for picnic.

Fruit Kabobs

Ingredients

1 pint strawberries, halved
1 to 2 oranges, wedged
1 lb bag grapes, red/purple
1 to 2 kiwis, sliced
pineapple, chopped

Directions

I.   Skewer fruit, alternating one kind of fruit to another.
II.   Add completed fruit kabobs to freezer-safe Ziploc® bags, (do not freeze them).
III. Add the bags to a cooler before going out for a picnic.

Smokey BLT

Ingredients

4 tbsp mayo, rosemary
8 slices bread, country (4 sandwiches)
5 oz cheese, smokey blue
¼ head lettuce, romaine
2 lg tomatoes, beefsteak

Directions

I. Spread rosemary mayo over the bread on one side and add meat and cheese.
II. Layer sandwiches with lettuce and tomato.
III. Slice and wrap the sandwiches in sandwich paper or Tupperware and chill in fridge until ready for the picnic.

Hot Chicken Peppered Sandwiches

Ingredients

2 chicken breasts, skinless, boneless
3 tbsp lemon, juice
1/8 cup oil, olive
3 tsp rosemary
1 tsp salt and pepper to taste
1/2 cup mayo
3 oz hot salami
1 cup hot peppers, pickled
6 oz cheese, fontina
4 bagels

Directions

I.   Marinate chicken with lemon juice and seasonings in a shallow pan for about 1 1/2 hrs in the fridge.
II.   Preheat oven to 400 °F and roast chicken for about 25 to 30 minutes.
III. Remove chicken from the oven and thinly slice.
IV.   Prepare the sandwiches by adding remaining ingredients to sliced bagels.

Tropical Rice with Fruit Salad

Ingredients

1 cup rice, black
¾ tsp salt
2 cups mango, cubes
1 ½ cups papaya, cubes
2 avocadoes
½ onion, chopped
2 tbsp lemon, juice
3 tbsp oil, olive
salt and pepper to taste

Directions

I.   Boil 2 cups water and add the black rice and ¾ tsp salt. Cook for about 25 to 30 minutes, drain.
II.   Add the remaining ingredients, toss and stir well so that they are well-combined.
III. Add to Tupperware container or other picnic-friendly container with a lid.

Celery and Apple Slaw

Ingredients

½ cup mayo
2 tsp tarragon, chopped
1 tsp lemon, zest
½ tsp salt
2 tbsp horseradish, grated
2 tbsp lemon, juice
2 bulbs celery root
2 apples

Directions

I. Stir together the first three ingredients with the horseradish in a small-to-medium size bowl.
II. In a separate bowl, combine the remaining ingredients and stir into the mayo-blend bowl.
III. Add to a picnic-friendly container.
IV. Let it sit for about 45 minutes to an hour before serving.

Sweet and Tangy Melon Salad

Ingredients

4 tbsp shallots, chopped
4 tbsp mint, chopped
¼ cup vinegar, cider
2 tbsp honey
1 tsp salt and pepper to taste
1 pear
½ cucumber, sliced
1 jicama, shredded
1 ½ cup watermelon, chopped

Directions

I.   Whisk everything but the fruit and jicama together in a bowl, making sure everything is well blended.
II.   Add in the fruits and jicama and toss well.
III.   Chill for about 1 to 2 hours before adding to a picnic-friendly container or serving.

Picnic Pineapple Drink

Ingredients

1 lg pineapple
1 ½ cups sugar
11 sprigs lavender
¼ cup lemon, juice

Directions

I.   Prepare the pineapple by cutting, peeling and throw away the core. Cut into 1" to 2" slices.
II.   Add the fruit to a blender or food processor and blend until fruit is crushed. Do not puree.
III.   Pour fruit into a large pot and add in remaining ingredients.
IV.   Bring the ingredients to a boil, then reduce to a simmer for about 12 to 15 minutes.
V.   Strain the drink to get rid of any unnecessary pieces of lavender.
VI.   Pour into a thermos or a large pitcher for a picnic and chill.

Macaroni Salad

Ingredients

1 lb macaroni, elbow
2 oz prosciutto, sliced
1 shallot, minced
¼ cup vinegar, red wine
1 tsp mustard, Dijon
½ cup EVOO
1 tomato, chopped
½ cup cheese, goat, crumbled
¼ cup olives, Cerignola
2 tbsp capers
¼ cup parsley, chopped

Directions

I. Boil water and cook the pasta according to the package, strain and set aside.
II. In a skillet, cook the prosciutto until crispy, drain the fat.
III. Combine the other ingredients in a bowl, then stir in the prosciutto.
IV. Pour the pasta into the tomato sauce and toss.
V. Season with parsley, salt and pepper to taste.
VI. Cool to room temperature and store in a picnic-friendly container.

Strawberry Lemonade

Ingredients

1 pint strawberries
8 tbsp + 2 tsp sugar
8 tbsp lemon, juice
water, seltzer

Directions

I.   Puree the stemmed strawberries, add 2 tsp sugar in a food processor or blender.
II.   Add 3 tbsp of the strawberry blend into each of two glasses.
III.   Add 4 tbsp sugar and 4 tbsp lemon juice into each glass.
IV.   Stir the blends in each glass and pour seltzer water into each glass, add ice to taste.
V.   Season to taste with more sugar as wanted or needed.

Lemon Sweet Tea

Ingredients

8 cups water
4 tea bags
¾ cup sugar
lemon, sliced

Directions

I.   Boil 3 cup water, remove from the heat and add in the tea bags.
II.   Let the tea steep for about 6 to 7 minutes.
III.   Throw away the tea bags and pour the warm water and sugar into a large pitcher.
IV.   Stir until the sugar has dissolved completely.
V.   Stir in the remaining 5 cups of cold water and mix well.
VI.   Pour into a picnic-friendly pitcher or thermos.

Pink Palmer Jars

Ingredients

1 pitcher lemonade
1 pitcher tea, green
mint, sprigs

Directions

I.   Blend the two pitchers into one large pitcher and pour into an equal number of mason jars.
II.   Add jars to a cooler with ice.

Picnic Mango Tea

Ingredients

1 mango, ripe, pitted and chunked
2 cups strawberry, sliced
1 cup sugar
1 cup tea, peppermint
1 lemon
5 cups black tea, cold water

Directions

I.   Add the mango, strawberries and sugar to a blender.
II.   Pour in the peppermint and black tea and blend
        everything until smooth.
III.   Juice the lemons, remove the seeds and add the lemon
        juice to the blender, blend one more time until everything
        is smooth.
IV.   Add tea to mason jars with lids or a large picnic-friendly
        thermos or pitcher.
V.   Store in a cooler with ice until ready to serve.

Made in the USA
Monee, IL
29 February 2020

22516550R00017